T0360984

Routledge Library Editions

BRITAIN IN THE
WORLD ECONOMY

ECONOMICS

INTERNATIONAL ECONOMICS
In 11 Volumes

BRITAIN IN THE WORLD ECONOMY

DENNIS H ROBERTSON

Routledge
Taylor & Francis Group

LONDON AND NEW YORK

First published in 1954

Reprinted in 2003 by
Routledge
2 Park Square, Milton Park, Abingdon, Oxon, OX14 4RN

Transferred to Digital Printing 2007

Routledge is an imprint of the Taylor & Francis Group

All rights reserved. No part of this book may be reprinted or reproduced
or utilized in any form or by any electronic, mechanical,
or other means, now known or hereafter invented, including photocopying
and recording, or in any information storage or retrieval system, without
permission in writing from the publishers.

The publishers have made every effort to contact authors/copyright holders
of the works reprinted in *Routledge Library Editions – Economics*. This has
not been possible in every case, however, and we would welcome
correspondence from those individuals/companies we have been unable to
trace.

These reprints are taken from original copies of each book. In many cases
the condition of these originals is not perfect. The publisher has gone to
great lengths to ensure the quality of these reprints, but wishes to point
out that certain characteristics of the original copies will, of necessity, be
apparent in reprints thereof.

British Library Cataloguing in Publication Data
A CIP catalogue record for this book
is available from the British Library

Britain in the World Economy
ISBN 0-415-31363-5
ISBN-0-415-31355-4

Miniset: International Economics

Series: Routledge Library Editions – Economics

Britain in the World Economy

SIR DENNIS H. ROBERTSON

Professor of Political Economy
Fellow of Trinity College, Cambridge

The Page-Barbour Lectures for 1953
at the
University of Virginia

Routledge
Taylor & Francis Group

LONDON AND NEW YORK

FIRST PUBLISHED IN 1954

This book is copyright under the Berne Convention. Apart from any fair dealing for the purposes of private study, research, criticism or review, as permitted under the Copyright Act 1911, no portion may be reproduced by any process without written permission. Enquiry should be made to the publisher.

PREFACE

THESE lectures were written for oral delivery on March 17–20, 1953, at the University of Virginia. Any English reader, finding much that is over-familiar to him, is invited to remember that the audience was American; and any reader who happens to be an economist is invited to remember that it was largely non-specialist.

Events move rapidly in this field; and in preparing the lectures for print I have not attempted to bring them up to date. In one respect, however, they had to be delivered at a particularly unfortunate moment, since the mass of statistical information which becomes available on and around Budget Day in England was not to hand. I have therefore modified, in the light of later information, the somewhat over-pessimistic figures about private saving which I put before my audience in Lecture I, and have added a statistical note showing the basis of the revised calculations.

I have thought it unnecessary and inexpedient to pepper the text with footnotes, as though it purported to be a serious piece of economic research. I should like, however, to make a general preliminary acknowledgment of the main sources of my pilferings.

In Lecture I, I have built largely on an article on "British Economic Policy, 1946–50," by Prof.

Preface

E. A. G. Robinson, in *The London and Cambridge Economic Service Bulletin*, May 1950, and on one on "The Outlook for British Industry," by Prof. G. C. Allen, in *The Westminster Bank Review*, August 1952. And I have followed the main structure of my own article on "British National Investment Policy," printed in *Utility and All That, and Other Essays* (Allen & Unwin, 1952).

In Lecture II, I have made much use of *The Sterling Area*, by Mr. A. R. Conan (Macmillan & Co.), and of published and unpublished writings on the same theme by Mr. J. O. N. Perkins of Cambridge.

In Lecture III, I have derived stimulus from many sources, but mainly, I think, from Dr. C. F. Kindleberger's *Dollar Shortage* and Mrs. Honor Croome's article "The Dollar Siege" (*Lloyds Bank Review*, July 1950).

In Lecture IV, I have built on the masterly treatment by Prof. J. Viner in *The Customs Union Issue* (Carnegie Endowment for International Peace, 1950), as amplified and amended in an equally masterly review by Prof. J. E. Meade in *Economica*, May 1951.

Finally, I would like to offer my warmest thanks to the Trustees of the Page-Barbour Foundation for giving me the opportunity to visit Charlottesville, and to all those whose kindness, hospitality and encouragement contributed to make my visit such an extremely delightful experience.

CAMBRIDGE   D. H. ROBERTSON

August 1, 1953

CONTENTS

I

The Mother Country

IN preparing to take advantage of the profound honour which you have done me in asking me to deliver the Page-Barbour Lectures at this ancient and beautiful University, I have had to face two great dilemmas. In the first place, you have invited an economist to follow a long line of distinguished scientists, historians, art-critics, poets. You have presumably done that with your eyes open, knowing economics to be a drab and crabbed specialism compared with most of those which occupy the attention of learned persons and fire the imagination of the intelligent public. But how am I to respond? How am I to steer a middle course between saying what will seem trite and trivial to those among my audience who are economists and saying what will seem dreary and incomprehensible to those who are not? I cannot tell whether or not I shall succeed in finding this middle way. But I would like to utter one word of encouragement and one of warning. I think there will be only one really difficult patch in what I have to say, and that will not be reached till the fourth lecture, when any survivors there may then be will have been well broken in. On the other hand, economics is, for good or evil, concerned with matters of greater and less, and though I am myself no mathematician or statistician, I cannot altogether let you off figures, which are nasty things to look at and still nastier to listen to. I think the worst concentration of them will occur in this first lecture, and if you can survive that, the rest will in this respect be easier on the ear and on the mind.

My other dilemma is this. I am to deal, if not, I hope, in a difficult manner, yet with difficult problems, which are the subject of controversy in my country and in yours, and sometimes between citizens of my country and citizens of yours. How freely am I to speak? It is bad manners, if one is asked out to dinner, to abuse one's host; and it is bad manners, of a rather subtler and more embarrassing kind, to abuse one's absent family in the presence of strangers. But good manners are not everything—there is also professional loyalty. I should feel professionally uneasy if I were to say in Charlottesville things which I would not say in Cambridge, and also if I were to refrain from saying in Charlottesville things which I *would* say if I were in Cambridge. I must ask you to accept the consequences in good part, without setting me down in thought either as an enemy of your country or as a traitor to my own.

In this first lecture I have to try to paint a picture of the post-war economic situation of Britain herself. There are many ways in which one might approach this task, some more picturesque than others. I have chosen a very sober and unpicturesque way. I propose to make what I have to say hang round one very prosaic thread—the state of the country in respect of its equipment of physical capital.

I must start therefore with some rather dull and also highly uncertain figures, which will all be expressed in pounds sterling. It has been estimated that at the end of 1945 the internal capital equipment of the United Kingdom was worth about 25 billion, and that a shrewd observer at that date would have seen that we needed to make, over the next few years at the then current price-level, expenditures of some 4½ billion in order to bring it back to its pre-war state, one-third of this being required to make good actual war destruction, and two-thirds to make up for arrears of maintenance and replacement. To this he might have felt disposed to add another 2½ billion, making 7 in all, in order to keep pace with the growth of population and of industrial employment.

How nearly had we achieved this result by the end of 1951, where the official figures stop? It is impossible to say with any precision. In those six years, apart from making some current repairs to works and buildings, we had spent nearly 9 billion on fixed capital objects of one kind and another, or about one-seventh of our gross product during the period. But how much of this was necessary to keep us from falling still further behind and how much represented a contribution towards getting back to the pre-war position it is impossible to say; and our official statisticians have now apparently given up the attempt. If we could assume that the sums actually exempted from income taxation as being needed to prevent us from slipping backwards were in fact sufficient for that purpose, we could conclude that 6 out of the 9 billion represented a net increase of capital wealth. But we certainly cannot make that assumption, for in a time of rapidly rising prices these depreciation allowances, being reckoned on the original cost of capital plant, become gravely insufficient to finance its replacement at current costs. Guessing at the effect of that complication as best one can, I suspect that the true figure for net addition to our fixed capital in 1946–51 is not above 5 billion. To this we can add about 1 billion spent over the period in replenishing our stocks of working capital, that is to say, useful goods in store and in process, this figure being the net result of some heavy swings in both directions. But since most of this expenditure, both on fixed and working capital, was made at prices higher than those prevailing in 1946, we must write our total of 6 billion down again say to 5 before comparing it with the 7 which our shrewd observer in 1946 would have discerned as necessary to equip our industrial population per head as well as it had been equipped before the war. And in 1952 we had to allow such running down of certain stocks, and impose such checks on expenditure on equipment, that I doubt if we shall be found to have made, on the same scale of reckoning, as much as another 1 billion of progress. It is not easy to regard this as a very satisfactory conclusion; though it is not, I think, a disgraceful one.

So much for the *amount* of our post-war capital outlay; now what about its *character?* Three questions arise, which are partly interconnected, but which I must try to separate out and to treat in order. First, has the distribution between what may broadly be called industrial purposes on the one hand and social and administrative purposes on the other been appropriate, having regard to our impoverishment by the war and to the extent to which we have relied on foreign loans and gifts for the means to execute the programme? Secondly, has the composition of the industrial part of the programme been appropriate to the particular economic problems with which we have been faced? Thirdly, have the methods by which the programme has been financed been consistent with economic health, or is there reason to fear that they have impaired in any way the springs of further progress?

About the first question the official statisticians are able to tell us quite a lot for the last four years of the period, 1948 to 1951. Of the gross expenditure of about 6½ billion pounds on fixed capital objects in these years, roughly one-quarter can be classed as social and administrative, three-quarters as industrial in the broad sense; of the former, three-quarters was on new houses, mostly built by local governments and heavily subsidised, the rest on schools, hospitals, drains, Government offices and so forth. It is difficult to form a judgment as to whether these proportions are reasonable without knowing, in respect of each of the two broad sectors, how much is to be regarded as replacement and how much as a true net addition to the wealth existing at the beginning of the period; and that, as I said just now, is just what is so difficult to tell. Suppose, for instance, we were able to regard the whole of the social quarter, which is nearly all building, as being additional wealth, and the industrial three-quarters, which consisted largely of the relatively short-lived items of plant, machinery and vehicles, as having been required to the extent of a half for replacement purposes. We should then conclude that the net additions to social wealth and industrial wealth had been in about the proportion of two to three. That might well seem a somewhat extravagant distribution of effort for a country in our position, even when we recall that nearly half a million houses, or about one in every twenty-eight of the pre-war number, were destroyed or rendered uninhabitable by enemy action, and also that since the war there has been a remarkable, and on the whole welcome, increase in the number of children requiring shelter and instruction.

Such a calculation, however, would be somewhat misleading, for this reason. Buildings, even when given a certain amount of current repair, *are* subject to obsolescence and decay, though taxing authorities are sometimes slow to recognise the fact. In particular, it seems clear that the whole of the new housing units, now approaching 1 ½ million, turned out in Britain since the war cannot be regarded as a net addition to this form of social wealth; for the condition of many old houses has been getting steadily worse, and it is even being alleged, though this is certainly an exaggeration, that old houses are now falling out of use as fast as new ones are being built, that is, at the rate of more than 200,000 a year. This regrettable state of affairs is due primarily to a preposterous tangle of rent restriction laws, which render it unprofitable, and indeed impossible, for many private owners of house property to keep it in proper repair, and which incidentally inflate the total demand for house-room by destroying the incentive to tenants to move out of quarters which are bigger than they need. The Churchill Government, while it has modified somewhat the perfectionist standards of public house-building previously in vogue, has, in glaring contrast to its general policy of temporarily damping down capital outlay, stuck to its determination to outdo its predecessor in respect of the number of new houses annually built. But it has so far made no more effort than its predecessor did to arrest the decay of existing houses by recasting the rent restriction laws, though we have been told recently that the whole matter is now under consideration. Whether or not our total national expenditure on housing has been excessive, its distribution between new building and repair is, I think, certainly open to criticism.

Now for my second question. Given the size of

our total capital outlay, and given its distribution between industrial and social purposes, has the 75 per cent devoted to industry been wisely distributed between different uses? That question has to be examined in relation to the main problem which Britain has had to face since the war, which is of course connected with the change in her overseas position. It is, in a way, the exact opposite of the problem with which she was faced in the inter-war period. In those days she was able to pay for a fifth of her imports out of the income derived from her foreign investments; and she was getting the remainder at a price, in terms of her exports, much lower—in 1938, 30 per cent lower—than she had had to pay in 1913. Her governmental expenditure overseas was very moderate, and she had ceased to strive to add to her foreign investments. Her problem was so to modify the direction of her economic effort as to reap the improvement in her standard of life which this relatively easy overseas position theoretically put within her grasp. It was a problem partly solved by a great wave of house-building and a great expansion of miscellaneous consumption and service trades, but partly left unsolved; for the transfer of effort proved too difficult to effect quickly on the requisite scale, and much of the potential improvement went to waste in the form of derelict industrial areas and chronically unemployed labour.

The war left us in a completely changed situation. In the first place, we found ourselves faced with a bill for military and other official expenditure overseas which, while it has since been somewhat reduced, bears an enormously greater proportion to our national income than before the war. Secondly, we found ourselves paying for our imports at a price, in terms of our exports, which in 1947 was already 15 per cent higher (by 1951 it had risen to be over 40 per cent higher) than in the pre-war decade. Thirdly, this same rise in import prices meant that even if our net income from overseas investment had remained unchanged in money terms, it would have been paying in 1947 for no more than two-fifths of the old volume of imports. But fourthly, we had had to sell £1 billion of overseas investments and incur £3 billion of overseas debt, so that the money value of our net income from overseas investment had itself been halved. Finally, this change in our overseas capital position made it desirable to do something, as soon as we could, towards repaying our overseas debt and rebuilding our stock of overseas income-yielding investments.

All these changes pointed in the same direction—to a need to reverse sharply the partial readjustment that had been made in the 1930s, and to re-orient our economy towards making a higher proportion of its product available for export. This would have been difficult enough if we had been starting from the 1938 level. But in point of fact, as a result of the concentration of our war-effort on the production of armies and armaments—a concentration rendered possible by the receipt of lend-lease aid—our exports had sunk by the end of the war to a level only 30 per cent of that of 1938. Whatever criticism some of us, at home or abroad, may be inclined to make of the post-war behaviour of the British people and of its Government, I do not think it can be denied that the raising of our exports by 1951 to 180 per cent of their 1938 volume—six times their volume of 1944—represents a very remarkable achievement, which some of us at the end of the war would scarcely have thought to be possible. At the same time our sadly depleted merchant fleet has been so fully brought up to strength that our net shipping earnings suffice to pay for a packet of imports substantially greater than before the war. And in our endeavour to pay our way, this expansion of the earnings side of the account has been accompanied by measures which, crude and unsatisfactory as we may feel them to be, have succeeded, except in 1951, in keeping the volume of imports to be paid for at well below its pre-war level.

It is in the light of its contribution to these overriding purposes that our post-war pattern of industrial investment must be scrutinised. If much has been achieved, could more have been achieved by a better-balanced development? Here are the outstanding facts, as recorded by the official statisticians. Of that 75 per cent of total investment which was devoted to industrial purposes in 1948–51, general manufacturing accounts for 30, transport (including shipping) for 15, electricity and gas for 10, agriculture for 5, leaving 15 for a number of other activities, including coal-mining and the building industry itself.

In looking at these proportions, we are met once more by the difficulty of determining how much of the gross outlay in each sector represents mere replacement and how much a net addition to capital wealth. It seems clear that the replacement element is likely to be specially high in the sector of general manufacture; and it is a common complaint among British industrialists that, allowance being made for this, general industry has been starved in favour of the great nationalised public utilities and of certain other so-called "basic" industries which, whether nationalised or not, are supposed to have been specially well placed for exercising a pull on the controlling authorities in Whitehall. I cannot claim to have an intimate enough knowledge of British industry to be able to form a reliable independent judgment on the validity of these complaints. There are certain facts about the sources of the saving embodied in the programme of capital investment which give them a certain plausibility, and to which I shall be turning in a moment. There is one great nationalised concern, the British Electricity Authority, which appears to me to have made, and to be still making, an excessive claim on the national savings, as a result of a persistent refusal to charge prices for its juice which cover its true cost of production, and especially to experiment with systems of charging which would discourage excessive consumption by domestic consumers at peak hours. In the case of coal, and of iron and steel, the scale of capital outlay does not seem to have been in itself excessive, having regard to the basic importance of both industries to the national economy and especially to the export effort. What is disappointing in the case of coal is the meagre results in the way of increased output so far achieved; and what is doubtful, in both cases, is whether the capital sums expended have always been laid out to the best advantage, and have not sometimes been unduly deflected, for social-political reasons, to keeping alive elderly and unsuitable centres of production, instead of being concentrated on developing more promising ones. It must be remembered, however, that when an economy is very short of investable resources, there is more than at first meets the eye to be said for hand-to-mouth schemes of patching as compared with technically more attractive plans which would take a long time to come to fruition.

Within the general objective of improving the country's external balance of payments there is a further distinction to be drawn—namely, between effort devoted to the expansion of exports and effort devoted to the replacement of imports. Has the balance between these two sub-ends been held about right? Perhaps we shall never know for certain, at any rate not for fifty years. In two fields in particular, the production of food and the refinement of petroleum, policy and therefore capital outlay have been deliberately steered in the direction of making Britain more nearly self-sufficient. As regards oil-refining, the antics of Dr. Mossadeq have gone far to justify retrospectively what might have seemed at one time—I confess it did to me—a somewhat over-ambitious programme. As regards agriculture, the present aim is to expand the production of food to a level 60 per cent above pre-war—a level representing some three-fifths instead of two-fifths of our total food consumption. This policy rests on the belief that, while there may from time to time still be gluts of particular foodstuffs, the relative rise in the world price of food as compared with manu-factured products has come to stay, so that to adapt our economy to this lasting change is not an act of wanton autarcism but only of reasonable fore-sight. On the whole I share this view, though in my country, as in others I could name, the political and emotional forces on the side of agricultural pro-tectionism are so strong that I feel sure they need watching, lest they land us in a position of such rigidity as to prevent us from taking advantage of such technical improvements in agricultural pro-ductivity overseas as Nature and Art may surely still have in store. It seems too that the methods by which our agricultural expansion has been secured may need some overhaul. In this respect our late planning Government displayed, somewhat para-doxically, a touching faith in the efficacy of the price mechanism, and proceeded, by a generous system of guaranteed prices, to pour into the pockets of the farming community a stream of money income which by 1950 was nearly five times its pre-war size, in the hope, which has not perhaps been more than partially fulfilled, that the lion's share of the increase in *real* income which this figure denotes would be channelled back into the land. And there does not seem much doubt that security of tenure for the farmer has now become so great as to hinder in many cases the passage of land into the hands best qualified to make full use of it.

On the side of export promotion, it may perhaps be said that the proof of the pudding is in the eating —that the pattern of capital outlay has been such as to render possible both that 80 per cent increase in the volume of exports to which I have already alluded and the striking change which has come about in its composition. Two-fifths of our exports now consist of machinery, vehicles and electrical goods, as compared with one-quarter before the war; while the share of cotton and wool has shrunk from one-sixth to one-ninth (in 1913 it had been nearly one-third). On the other hand, it must be conceded, first, that the foundations for this change had largely been laid already during the war itself, by the expansion of the metal industries for purposes of munition-making; and secondly, that even now it has probably not gone far enough. On the positive side, it may be argued that more could have been done at various times to channel precious supplies of steel into the expanding and exchange-earning motor-car and shipbuilding industries; on the negative side, that it was unwise of the late Government, if it was prepared to give a special subsidy to capital outlay in any privately-owned industry, to select one whose long-run prospects are so dubious, and which has shown so little power or will to change its ways, as the Lancashire cotton industry. In the main, however, policy has supported a change in the character of Britain's export effort which has been inexorably dictated by world conditions, but which nevertheless brings fresh anxieties in its train. For in the first place, owing to this new concentration on the export of metal goods, there is now sharper competition than of old between the claims made by export markets and the claims made by the modernisation of industrial plant at home on metal supplies and on engineering skill; and in the last two years there has entered into that competitive struggle a third hungry claimant in the shape of a formidable programme of rearmament. Secondly, in many of the new or expanded lines of export British industry is now more directly in competition with the gigantic industry of America and the rapidly reviving industry of Germany than of old; a certain comfortable specialisation between the three countries which had worked itself out in the inter-war period has been disrupted by the war. Thirdly, remembering the special force with which in the past cyclical depression has hit the industries making instrumental or constructional goods, it is not altogether pleasant to reflect that our power of earning our food has become more dependent than before on the maintenance of world demand for precisely these categories of products.

Britain in the World Economy

I come now to the third and last of the questions which I distinguished. Have the means by which this capital outlay has been financed been such as to give cause for anxiety for the future? To drive home the points I want to make I shall give you some figures for one year only, 1951, with the warning, or reassurance, first, that they contain a good deal of guess-work, and secondly, that they are considerably more spectacular, and indeed alarming, than would be the average figures for the whole post-war period, or, let us hope, those for 1952.[1] In 1951, the recorded gross outlay at home for purposes of a capital nature was about £3,225 million; but of this total £900 million is bogus—it represents simply the enhancement in money value, during a period of rapidly rising prices, of unchanged volumes of physical stocks of goods in store or in process. From the remaining £2,325 million let us knock off £875 million as representing the cost of keeping our fixed capital equipment from shrinking (that is a deduction rather greater than the taxation authorities admitted to be necessary for the purpose, but I think most people would agree that it is by no means too large). This leaves some £1,450 million as the true value of the extensions and improvements made in our capital stock at home. Who did the saving which was embodied in these extensions and improvements?

Well, nearly 30 per cent of it was done, not by ourselves at all, but by members of other nations—

[1] See Statistical Note at end of Lecture I.

only a little of it, in this particular year, by way of gift, most of it by putting money in our banks, buying our Government securities, or taking over the gold which we unloaded out of our reserves. This was a shaming state of affairs, which we are agreed must not occur again; we have to rebuild those reserves, and to make what contribution we can—it cannot, in my view, at present be great—to the creation of capital wealth overseas, rather than call on other people to help us in creating it in our own island.

What of the remaining savings, say £1,035 million, which were made at home? Who made them and how? Some £575 million of them were made by the Government, out of the proceeds of taxes and levies of various kinds. This is a very remarkable and, if it could be taken by itself, might be regarded as a very encouraging fact. Most people, I think, even ten years ago would have expressed grave doubts whether any democratically elected government would ever be prepared to make provision for the future on so large a scale. It is above all to one man, that austere dedicated figure Sir Stafford Cripps, that we owe the demonstration that in actual fact, and not merely in paper exercises, budget surpluses can be an important instrument of saving.

The obverse of the picture is less reassuring. We have, you will remember, £1,035 million of net saving done within the country to track to its sources. We have found that £575 million was provided by Government action. The next thing we find is that private persons and corporations set aside some £520 million to pay the additional taxes arising on their currently earned income but not falling to be paid till a later date. From some points of view it seems more illuminating to count these sums as Government-engineered saving rather than as true private saving. But if we do this, what do we find? We find that Government-engineered saving, at nearly £1,100 million, exceeded total home saving by £65 million, in other words, that what we may call unencumbered private saving was a negative figure of appreciable size.

On my assumptions, 1951 was the first year, and let us hope it will prove to have been the last, of which this was true of private saving taken as a whole. But it was by no means the first year of which it was true of the savings of *individuals*, including in that term farmers and other owners of unincorporated businesses. There seems to be no doubt that for some years individual saving, even if we include additions made to tax-reserves, has been running at a substantial negative figure, the savings of those who save being insufficient to make up for the amount by which other people are drawing on their capital, whether to pay death duties, etc. (amounting to some £200 million a year), to finance the education of their children or for other less laudable purposes. But in 1948–50 this individual dissaving had been outweighed by unencumbered savings by corporations out of their undistributed profits—

savings which, while much smaller than the corporations would have liked to make and much smaller than those effected through the machinery of taxation, had nevertheless averaged some £375 million a year.

How far has this distortion, by pre-war standards, in the *sources* of saving been responsible for a distortion in the *uses* of saving? That is a disputed question to which in the nature of things no precise answer can be given. Every company chairman is of course acutely aware of the huge taxes he has been paying, not only on his genuine profits, but on the fictitious accounting profits resulting, during a period of inflation, from increases in the prices of his stock-in-trade and in the replacement costs of his machinery and plant. He is naturally inclined to assume that if he had not been mulcted in these taxes he could have expanded and modernised his plant to a much greater extent than he has done, and that the country would have been better equipped in consequence to meet the competitive struggle which now lies before it. But given the Government's general investment plans, and the shortages of steel, timber and other materials which have prevailed through most of the period, there is a limit to the extent to which merely to have left the corporations in possession of more of their own money would have changed the outcome. The retained sums might merely have competed with one another to send the prices of materials rocketing upwards, or have perforce remained unspent and been offered, directly or indirectly, to the Government to finance those programmes of housing and so forth which it has in fact financed out of its budget surpluses.

Nevertheless, I am myself strongly of the opinion that our present pattern of saving is fraught with danger for the future. There are, it is true, drawbacks as well as advantages in the unlimited ploughing back into their own businesses of the profits made by strong and established companies. That may tend towards elephantiasis; in principle it may be better that such concerns should submit their schemes of expansion to the arbitrament of the market by placing new issues. But that alternative depends on the existence of a class of private savers able and willing to take industrial risks; and it is precisely the virtual disappearance of that class which is one of the causes for disquiet. The greater part of the individual saving still done in my country is done in the form of insurance premiums and other risk-shunning instruments of investment. And when we turn from the large to the small business, whether yet incorporated or not, there seems to me no doubt that the difficulty which present levels of taxation place in the way of such a business growing by means of its own savings hangs as a question-mark, if not as a cloud, over the future of British industry

One is often driven to wonder whether, in respect of business leadership though not of material wealth, we have not in these post-war years been living on our capital. Those now at the head of the great British business enterprises go on giving of their best in the changed environment in which they find themselves—what else, especially at a time of national stress and difficulty, should they do? But they are ageing and will pass away—who will succeed them? There is perhaps more interest than ever before in providing ladders for ability and organising management as a skilled profession. But whether, as a breeding-ground for the highest industrial leadership, such things can be made a satisfactory substitute for the new firm fighting its way to the front and feeding on its own saved profits in the way that used to be so common and has now become so difficult, remains to be seen.

If they can, Britain's geographical advantages are still there; so is the scientific and inventive genius which has flowered forth in penicillin and the Comet and the atomic pile; so is the solidity of character and the manual skill. And there is much, in the way of improved health and nutrition of the rising generation of workers, to be set to the credit of the so-called Welfare State. Is the climate of opinion such as to permit the most effective utilisation of these precious ingredients? Or has the weight and complexity of the social and administrative structure which British industry is expected to carry on its back become too great? The future alone can reveal the answer.

STATISTICAL NOTE TO LECTURE I

The calculations towards the end of this lecture have been revised in the light of the revised estimates contained, together with provisional estimates for 1952, in the Government White Paper Cmd. 8803. Working on the lines explained in the text, we now obtain the following figures:

	£ million		
	Average 1948–50	1951	1952
Apparent gross home investment	1989	3227	1900
Less stock appreciation	—417	—900	—
True gross home investment	1572	2327	1900
Less estimated depreciation	—711	—873	—958
Estimated true net home investment	861	1454	942
Less savings contributed from overseas or		—420	
plus investment abroad	49		266
Home saving	910	1034	1208
Less estimated true Government saving	—702	—575	—405
Less additions to private tax reserves	—96	—522	—98
Net private 'unencumbered' saving	112	—63	705
Of which done by companies and public corporations	374	185	651
Remainder done by persons	—262	—248	54
after meeting death duties and other capital taxes	220	194	159
i.e. gross personal "unencumbered" saving	—43	—54	213

It will be seen that, as foreshadowed in the lecture, the position as regards private savings became considerably more favourable in 1952.

Technical Notes

1. In allocating stock appreciation between the various parties, I have based myself on the treatment by F. W. Paish in *District Bank Review*, March 1953.

2. My figure for depreciation is arrived at by adding the official figures for Central and Local Governments, farmers and professional persons to 1½ times the figure for *normal* allowances to private traders and companies and 1½ times that for public corporations, and ignoring "initial allowances". This is, of course, no more than a wild guess.

3. In the official arrangement (Cmd. 8803, table 6), taxes on capital are excluded from the Government contribution to the finance of investment, and included in that of private persons (as in the last line of my table).

The Sterling Area

In the general sketch which I gave last time of Britain's progress since the war, I naturally had to say a good deal about her problems of overseas trade and payments. In this and the remaining lectures I want to concentrate more intensively on the problems of her external economic relations—with the other countries of the Commonwealth, with Europe, with the United States. It seems natural to begin by calling attention to the curious double position in which she finds herself as a country, so to speak, in her own right and as the centre of a group of countries now described in official language as the Scheduled Territories but commonly spoken of as the Sterling Area. This is both rather a tricky matter technically, and opens a window on to very large questions of political and economic policy.

What is the Sterling Area? The concept does not really go back beyond 1931; for before that date, so far as such a thing can now be seen in retrospect to have existed, it was more or less coterminous with the whole world. For many decades a very large proportion of the world's international trade had been invoiced in sterling, and a large proportion of the short loans needed to finance it had been put up by

London. Conversely, foreigners had often found it convenient not only to borrow from London but to lend to her, that is, to keep balances with English banks. Up to 1914, no foreigner had bothered to think whether what he was holding was just a pound sterling or a claim to so much gold; and no foreign Government which established a gold standard, as many did from 1870 onwards, bothered to think whether what it really wanted was to keep its money stable in terms of gold or in terms of sterling. And this whole set-up survived more or less unscathed the period from 1914 to 1925, when a balance in London was *not* in effect redeemable in a given amount of gold. Indeed, in one respect sterling in the 1920s became even more obviously the world's currency than ever before; for a number of countries, finding it expensive to keep reserves in gold against their local note-issues, took to following the example of India and keeping sterling balances, on which they could earn a little interest, instead. And this perhaps is a good moment to explain once for all that the term sterling balances, as commonly used, does not mean quite what it says; for it includes not only balances with banks but certain short-term investments, in particular holdings of the British Government's three-months Treasury Bills.

But after 1931, when the Bank of England was forced again to suspend gold payments, and the pound was allowed to depreciate in terms of gold and the dollar, a clear division began to emerge between three main groups of countries. First, there were the countries of Western Europe, which for long clung, with the aid of exchange-controls and import-restrictions of ever-increasing severity, to their old gold perches. Secondly, there was the United States, with the countries in her orbit, where President Roosevelt and his highbrow advisers proceeded to conduct a series of highly disturbing but not wholly unsuccessful experiments in monkeying about with the dollar-price of gold. And finally there were the countries which were either ordered to link their fortunes with the United Kingdom or, as heavy suppliers of the British market or keen competitors with British exporters, found it to their interest to do so. These countries so managed their affairs as to keep their currencies at parity with the pound sterling, and continued, in spite of the severe shock which they had suffered in 1931, to hold their currency reserves and their banking balances in London. In 1939 these balances amounted to about £500 million.

So was born the First Sterling Area—a motley group of countries bound together by certain common interests and habits, but without defined membership or formal rules or obligations. It may be said to have comprised not only most of the British Empire but also, among others, the Scandinavian countries, Argentina and Japan; but, it is most important to observe, *not* Canada, too closely bound to the American orbit to bring herself to hold balances in London or to permit her currency to follow sterling fully in its divergences from the United States dollar.

In the middle thirties, you will remember, the United States tied up again to gold; and since then the one really fixed point in the world's monetary affairs has been the declared willingness of the United States authorities to buy or sell gold, though only from or to foreign central banks and Treasuries, at the fixed price of $35 a fine ounce. During the last years of peace an incomplete and uneasy harmony between the monetary policies of the leading non-totalitarian countries was preserved by a mysterious instrument called the Tripartite Agreement. I have heard it irreverently referred to as the Tripe Agreement; but I must not stop to enter into its complexities, any more than into those of the Bretton Woods Agreements of 1944, of which it was in a sense the precursor.

With the outbreak of war in 1939, the composition and nature of the Sterling Area underwent a drastic change. The neutral countries fell away, all except Eire, still to this day, in spite of nationalist mutterings, too closely bound to the United Kingdom economy by her cattle and her investments to be anything but a member of the Area, though she cannot come to its parties but has to be asked to tea on a separate day. France had just been virtually incorporated by a mighty effort when she fell; but the scattered French colonies were members for a time, as were various other outlying parts of the world which got sucked into the war, some of which, such as Iceland, seem to have remained rather incongruously stuck to the fly-paper, while others eventually disappeared—it is a matter for casuistry whether Egypt, in 1947, withdrew with dignity or was kicked out. For most practical purposes we can think of the post-1939 Sterling Area as the British Commonwealth *plus* Eire *minus* Canada. And much more important than the subsequent comings and goings was the great change which was made in 1939 in the strength and nature of the cement binding the Area together.

For its mechanism was now to be used for the first time not merely as an instrument of war but, with more lasting effects, as an instrument of deliberate discrimination against certain products of certain not unfriendly countries. The urgent need was to conserve for essential uses both the stocks and the current earnings of the currencies of certain countries and of the gold which could purchase them. Some of these countries—Holland, Belgium, Norway—soon disappeared into Hitler's maw; others—Portugal, mother of sardines and wolfram, Argentina, breeder of beef—continued to give anxiety till the end, and sundry Orientals and others needed constant tipping in gold; but in the main the problem soon focused itself on the two North American dollars and the gold for which they could be bought. Nor did this problem vanish, though its urgency was much reduced, when American munitions and certain staple foods and raw materials came to be supplied on what turned out all right in the end to be gift terms, and when the expenditure of American troops in Britain and Australia enabled the United Kingdom to reconstitute her gold and dollar reserves from the vanishing-point to which it happened to be my own unpleasant duty to watch them melting away in the first eighteen months of war.

To conserve dollars the countries remaining in the Sterling Area instituted in 1939, under the leadership of the United Kingdom, a system of exchange control. It is important to be rather clear just what this meant, and still means, and what its bearing is on that ambiguous and inflammatory concept, the convertibility of the pound sterling. Consider first the position in the United Kingdom itself. Ever since 1931 the pound had been inconvertible in the sense that there was nobody from whom the owner of a bank balance in London had the right to demand gold at a fixed rate. But no such owner who wished to buy North American goods or securities was debarred from buying, at the price of the day as fixed in a large free market, the dollars required to pay for them; in *this* sense the pound had remained, even after 1931, freely convertible. Since 1939 there has been no free market, until the rudiments of one were restored eighteen months ago. Any resident owner or earner of dollars has had to turn them into a central pool, and any resident wanting dollars has had to ask for them out of the pool, with the knowledge that only for certain limited purposes and within certain strict limits of quantity is his request likely to be granted. But there is one respect in which the British system of exchange control differs from that which has been employed by some other countries. If the Englishman can show that he wants dollars to pay for an approved import he will get them without question; that is to say, the desired restriction of expenditure on dollar goods is secured, not at the money-issuing stage, but at an earlier stage, and is administered, not by the monetary authorities, but by the trade authorities. In this very limited sense the pound sterling has, even since 1939, remained convertible by United Kingdom residents. I shall have occasion in my last lecture to revert to this matter of technique.

Now let us turn to consider what the establishment of the new régime meant for the other countries of the Sterling Area. It meant first a position for the individual citizen *vis-à-vis* his Government similar to, though not, I think, always so strictly administered as, that in the United Kingdom; for the individual there was to be surrender of the proceeds of exports to dollar countries, restriction of the right to import goods costing dollars, abstention from capital investment outside the Sterling Area. But the system meant something more than this. It meant that each country *as a country* agreed to hand over its surplus dollar earnings to Mother in exchange for sterling, and to go to Mother when it wanted extra dollars to spend. Naturally the degree of confidence with which it exercised or presented claims on the dollar pool depended partly on its political status; the little black children, who were often the best earners, could be smacked on the head if they showed too great a propensity to spend dollars, while the grown-up white daughters, who were often pretty extravagant, could only be quietly reasoned with. And here it is necessary to mention the exception which proves the rule. South Africa, the great gold-producer, has never joined quite whole-heartedly in the pooling arrangements, and in 1948 withdrew from them altogether. More and more she has tended to pay for her own dollar needs, interpreted pretty generously, and to keep the bulk of her surplus gold output for herself; her sterling balances, while often of appreciable size, have never played the same dominant part in her system as Australia's and New Zealand's have in theirs. Nevertheless, both during and since the war she has sold Mother a great deal of gold in exchange for goods and securities, thus adding considerably to the strength of the dollar pool.

Taking account of gold production, the Outer Sterling Area during the war put several hundreds of millions of pounds more into the dollar pool than it took out—exactly how many hundreds has never, so far as I can discover, been revealed or perhaps even exactly calculated, but I think the answer is about $10\frac{1}{2}$, of which gold accounts for nearly 7. But the great growth in the Outer Area's holdings of sterling, from some £300 million at the end of 1939 to some £2,500 million at the end of 1945, was due also to another cause, much less clearly foreseen at the beginning of the war, but springing equally naturally out of the pre-war habits of the Area. This cause was simply the sale for pounds sterling to Mother herself, on an enormous scale, of goods and services for which, in the throes of war, she was in no position to supply goods and services in return. To take the leading example, of India's net earnings of sterling, three-fifths was due to reimbursement by the British Government of war expenditure incurred by the Government of India, mainly in rupees on the spot, and two-fifths to the sale of exports, both within and without the Sterling Area, by private traders. Of these earnings, after more than £300 million had been used for the repayment of long-term debt incurred over many decades, some £1,200 million appeared as sterling balances held by the Reserve Bank of India.

It should be noted that, so far as legal form goes, all the sterling balances of the Sterling Area countries remained immediately convertible into dollars, at the option of the authorities of the countries concerned, till well after the end of the war; and some of the most important are so still. But in 1947, after the premature attempt of the United Kingdom to restore a still wider measure of convertibility had ended in failure, formal agreements were made with India and the new State of Pakistan about the rate of which the balances could be drawn on both (*a*) for conversion into dollars and (*b*) for other purposes; and these arrangements, suitably recast so as to fit in with the programme for capital develop-

ment in South-East Asia known as the Colombo Plan,
still exist. The same process was applied to some
other countries, including Egypt when she slipped
or was pushed out of the Sterling Area, taking some
£350 million of sterling balances with her. And of
course the Colonial Governments have not been in a
position to exercise their legal rights in a manner
unduly embarrassing to Whitehall.

As I have indicated, the new Sterling Area in
battle-dress has outlasted the war, because the problem with which it was primarily formed to cope, the
mysterious disease called dollar shortage, is still
with us. But it has not survived without creaks and
groans; and the question can legitimately be raised
whether its continued existence is a good thing from
the point of view (*a*) of the United Kingdom, (*b*) of
the other constituent countries, (*c*) of the rest of the
world. I shall discuss this question today from the
two first points of view, promising to return later,
in a wider context, to the third. And first for a little
more potted history.

As the figures which I gave just now show, the
Sterling Area system was an immense source of
strength to the war effort of the United Kingdom;
it enabled her to borrow vast sums and to use a considerable portion of them for the most desired purpose, namely, the purchase of dollar goods. But
during the next four years, 1946–9, the boot was on
the other foot. Repaying debt is seldom such an
agreeable process as incurring it; and there was a
good deal of rather intemperate talk in England, by

politicians of both the leading parties and economists of diverse schools, about the flood of "unrequited exports" which was supposed to be pouring
into Asia in repayment of war debt incurred in her
defence, and to be causing an unwarranted strain on
Britain's productive capacity. What *is* certainly true
is that India, and most of the other major members of
the Outer Area except the gold-producers, dried up
as a source of dollar earnings and became instead a
source of dollar drain. Between them in those four
years they took about £600 million more out of the
dollar pool than they put into it, and thus took their
full share in causing that depletion of the Area's
gold and dollar reserves which pitched it—as I
think, about nine months too late—into devaluation
in September 1949.

After devaluation, and still more markedly after
the outbreak of the Korean War in June 1950, the
scene changed. The position in 1950, abnormal and
transitory as it turned out to be, illustrates so nicely,
if in exaggerated form, what Englishmen at least
like to think of as the normal working of the sterling
system, that it seems to me worth while bothering
you, in very round terms, with a few of the leading
figures, uncertain as some of them are. The United
Kingdom ran a deficit of £90 million with the dollar
area and a surplus of £260 million with its Sterling
Area partners. The latter, leaving out of account
what South Africa paid for with her own gold, ran
a surplus of £150 million with the dollar area and
sold £100 million of gold to the United Kingdom.

The Sterling Area

With the residue of the world, of which Western Europe forms the most important component, the United Kingdom ran a surplus of £130 million and the rest of the Area a surplus perhaps of £200 million. The net result of these transactions—to avoid confusing you I omit mention of various other things which were happening [1]—was to enable the United Kingdom to add £330 million to her gold and dollar reserves and to strengthen her banking position *vis-à-vis* the outside world in other ways by £160 million, though at the cost of adding £190 million to her banking debts to her sterling partners.

No wonder excited cries were heard from certain quarters in Washington to the effect that now at least dollar shortage could be regarded as an extinct disease, and Britain must modify her policies accordingly. No wonder that in Australia, become a net dollar earner for the first time in her peacetime history and contemplating with pride her golden fleeces, voices were heard questioning the whole basis of the Sterling Area system with its code of collective self-denial, and hinting that it was time that Old Mother Hubbard in London gave up the key of the cupboard, and allowed her daughters, or at least her *white* daughters, to set up house on their own.

But alas! never has the old tag *respice finem* been more dramatically justified. In 1951, as everybody

---

[1] Sundry gifts and capital transactions added another £245 million to the United Kingdom's gold and dollar reserves, and another £190 million to her banking liabilities to her Sterling Area partners.

43

knows, came another startling change of scene. The
soaring prices of Sterling Area products—wool, jute,
rubber, sisal—turned downwards towards the earth,
falling more sharply, what is more, than those of
the cereals, the cotton and the non-ferrous metals
emanating from the New World. Here, if you can
bear them, are a few more very round figures. In the
second half of 1951, the Outer Sterling Area's surplus with the dollar area and with the residue of the
outside world had been turned into deficits respec-
tively of £60 million and £170 million. In these six
months the daughters between them were not only
taking from Mother goods and services in excess of
what they sent to her valued at an annual rate of
£365 million, but were contributing at an annual
rate of £390 million to the weakening of her reserve
and banking position *vis-à-vis* the world outside the
family, which she herself was further impairing at
an annual rate of £1,150 million.

It is often difficult to redress one injury without
doing another; and many Englishmen who were
happily unconscious of the indirect harm which
Australia was doing to the British economy by in-
dulging in her spending spree became acutely conscious of the consequences when she decided to
bring it to an end, serving notice on Mother, quite
rightly but somewhat brusquely, that she could no
longer afford to waste her substance on prettily-
painted pottery and textiles or on smart motor-cars.
Anyway, it was now perhaps again the United Kingdom's turn to question whether the Sterling Area

system, drawing her into the very centre of the whirlwind which blows about the prices of primary products, is an unequivocal blessing.

I will not carry on the story through the painful readjustments of 1952, but will try to summarise. I am still, you will remember, looking at the Sterling Area system from the point of view of its own members, and asking how fairly it distributes among them the privileges and burdens of membership. I think the answer must be that there *is* no precise answer, and that in this as in other fields the awkward human passion for perfect distributive justice may lead us into a bog. Britain can argue in a general way that long ago, before dollar shortage was born or thought of, there had emerged a perfectly spontaneous pattern of triangular trade, under which she used her manufacturing skill to satisfy the carefully studied and well-understood needs of her daughters, while they found it perfectly convenient, out of the proceeds of the sale of their gold and raw produce, to help her to pay her dollar bills; that such a pattern should be helped to re-establish itself after the upsets of war is not therefore evidence of parasitism on her part or undue hardship for them. They in turn can point out that the survival of the old pattern depends on the continued ability of the mother-country to supply their needs efficiently, and that in point of fact they have sometimes found it difficult to get delivery from her, at reasonable prices and at due dates, of the things needed for their comfort and development.

Britain in the World Economy

At this point of the argument, if there is to be an argument, other elements can be brought in on both sides. The Antipodes can plead that they could have earned more dollars than they have done if they had not deliberately and in response to urgent requests channelled their food exports to the United Kingdom. The United Kingdom can urge that she has to bear the lion's share of the cost of imperial defence; Australia can reply that the feverish programme of immigration and construction which has made her such a big spender is really her contribution to the defence effort. India can argue that only by means of her lavish dollar expenditure and of those "unrequited exports" from Britain which Mr. Churchill and Mr. Dalton vied with one another in grudging her in 1947 was she able to avert famine and chaos and turn herself into the main bulwark against Communist engulfment of the East. Returning to the economic plane, Britain can point out that among the privileges of Sterling Area membership is access to the London capital market, and that as well as trying to repay her war-debts and in spite of acute capital shortage at home she has allowed her nationals since the war to invest several hundreds of millions of fresh money in the White Dominions.

My own feeling is that as between these White Dominions, the major Asiatic members and the mother-country the honours or dishonours have been about easy. All of them have sinned at one time or another in failing to control their own internal inflations. All of them are now trying to do

46

better, and to co-ordinate their efforts more closely with one another. None of them would be sensible to seek to quit or to disrupt prematurely a system which gives them all a certain amount of protection against the various vicissitudes to which they are severally subject.

There is, however, one important element in the sterling system of which a little more must be said. Taken as a group, the "dependent", that is to say not completely self-governing, members of the Area have been consistent breeders of dollars, generating a dollar surplus of £150 million in the bumper year 1950 and one of £50 million even in the black second half of 1951. Moreover, at first sight it would appear that these colonial peoples have not even been allowed to spend in sterling the equivalent of these dollar earnings; for between the end of 1945 and the middle of 1952 the sterling balances of the dependent territories increased from £450 million to £1,050 million. Is there here at least some ground for suspicion that the mother-country has been exploiting her trustee position, living for years in an odour of sanctity on the labours of the beneficiaries and promising to make it up to them some day? In the large and on the whole I do not think this suspicion is justified. There seems little doubt that in 1947 to 1949 the dependent territories were importing more goods and services from the rest of the world than they were exporting to it, and that both these import surpluses and the growth in their sterling balances were covered by an inflow of long-term capital from the United Kingdom, partly on Government and partly on private account. With the rise in prices and in the volume of trade since 1945, it is natural that these territories should require to keep larger currency reserves and banking balances in London; and as to their exceptional earnings in 1950, it would not have been true kindness to allow these simple peoples to dissipate them in the way that the sophisticated Australians chose to do. I do not think that on the whole it can be justly said that Britain has either unduly exploited or unduly neglected her colonial estate.

To this favourable verdict there are, however, I think, two qualifications to be made. First, with regard to one group of these territories, but one only, namely the West African colonies, a reasoned case has been put forward by reputable economists for the view that the policy of the official marketing boards in withholding from the individual cultivators of cocoa and vegetable oils the full benefits of high prices has been unduly rigid and puritanical, and suggestions have been made for the substitution of a more flexible system. This is a highly technical matter on which it is difficult to form a judgment, and I will say no more than that it is one to which the tag which I have already quoted, *respice finem*, is evidently highly relevant.

Secondly, there has undoubtedly been fumbling in the choice of instruments through which to make such investment as in her present circumstances Britain can afford to make in her colonial territory.

48

There is, of course, no necessary antithesis between development designed to raise the standard of life of backward peoples and development designed to furnish the rest of the world with food and materials which it needs; indeed, it is evident that the latter is the only sure and solid foundation for the former. An outstanding example of successful balance between the two objectives was furnished by British enterprise between the wars in the Gezira district of the Sudan, where there was evolved a system of partnership between the Sudan Government, a commercial company and the peasant cultivators of cotton which may well serve as a model for similar schemes in other lands. But the first post-war large-scale plan of development, the grandiose and ill-fated East African groundnuts scheme, initiated not by the Colonial Authorities but by the Ministry of Food, had the appearance at any rate of being unduly tilted in the direction of rapid exploitation of resources for the benefit of the stomachs of the Herrenvolk, and also exhibited numerous glaring faults of planning and execution. There seemed reason to hope more from the more modest and widely-diffused efforts of the Colonial Development Corporation, a body set up in 1948 and endowed with powers to borrow from the Government up to about £100 million for the purpose indicated in its title. But here also many of the earlier results were unfortunate. Here, in the pithy words of the new broom who took over the management in 1951, Lord Reith, is the story of the fate of one of its more ambitious enterprises—a gigantic poultry farm in Gambia: "(1) (*a*) In April 1951 there was an epidemic of Newcastle disease which wiped out the poultry flock; (*b*) that was the end of poultry-farming." And here, from the same pen, is a succinct statement of the dilemma with which the Corporation is faced. It was instructed, the writer says, "to do economic good: just that; but to do it without losing money." On that delicate task, like its wealthier companion in a wider field, the International Bank for Reconstruction and Development, it is still assiduously engaged.

The spotlight which has quite rightly been turned on these misadventures has perhaps unduly obscured the steady unspectacular progress which, with the aid of loans raised in London and of outright grants, now of some £20 million a year, made under the Colonial Welfare and Development Act, the several Colonial Governments have made with their own plans, and the parallel activities of the British overseas banking concerns and other private enterprisers. An official enquiry held last summer seems to have established that over the next two or three years it is not shortage of finance but partly of steel and partly of skilled labour and local organisation that stands in the way of more rapid progress. That is exactly what the International Bank found in its larger sphere. All experience seems to show that enthusiasts easily overrate the speed at which primitive societies can suck in large doses of imported capital without suffering grave attacks of economic and social indigestion.

Taking a longer view, however, there is no reason to doubt that the British colonial territories can gradually absorb a much larger intake of capital investment than has recently flowed to them and can make in return a much larger contribution to the world's flow of agricultural and mineral supplies. But in certain circles in my country there is a regrettable tendency to become confused about the time-order of these two processes. Those who are the most eloquent both about the limitless resources of the Colonial Empire and about the deplorably low standards of living of many of its 70 million inhabitants are often apt to be the least alive to the essential condition for exploiting the former and remedying the latter. That condition is the development, by increased production or reduced consumption at home, of a persistently favourable balance of payments by the mother-country. A somewhat belated discovery that, on a world scale of reckoning, the western urban trade unionist belongs to the over-privileged rather than the under-privileged classes is apt to fuse, in certain breasts, with an extreme unwillingness to surrender any improvement of standards once secured, and to generate a peculiarly woolly form of semi-philanthropic, semi-predatory pseudo-imperial mystique.

It sometimes nowadays needs saying that the West in general does not owe a living to societies which are unable to give themselves good government, to cultivate the simple virtue of thrift, and to cope with, or even to admit the existence of, their own overriding problem of excessive population growth. But it sometimes also needs saying in my country, especially perhaps in Lancashire, that if any section of the depressed populations of the world can find powerful friends who will help it and to whose prosperity it can contribute in return, such a section does not owe a living in perpetuity to that branch of the western world under whose political tutelage it happens to find itself. These amenities having been duly interchanged, it becomes possible to settle down to consider quietly what the possibilities are for all nations which are not set upon creating enmity and upheaval to co-operate in working out a relationship which, if not ideal for any, is yet tolerable for all. But that brings me face to face with a subject which I must reserve till next time—the relations between this Sterling Area whose internal problems I have tried to describe with some frankness and other countries, and particularly the relations between it and the United States of America.

III

Dollar Shortage

I HAVE left myself with a formidable bundle of promises to fulfil. We are to take another look at the Sterling Area, from outside instead of from within, and to glance at the commercial and financial relations of Britain with Western Europe and with North America. Evidently compression is necessary, and I must try to go straight to the heart of the matter.

The most convenient link between these various topics is to be found in the concept of dollar shortage, which in my last lecture I took for granted, but which I can now no longer evade examining. It is a concept which it is not at all easy to make precise. What it seems to mean is a persistent tendency on the part of the populations of the world outside North America to spend more in that region than the sum of what they are earning in that region and what the inhabitants of that region are disposed to lend to them or invest in their borders under the play of ordinary economic motive. The symptoms of the disease are a continuous pressure on the monetary reserves of the extra-North American countries, which is kept at bay partly by a series of special loans and gifts made to them by the North American countries, partly by special restrictions, imposed on themselves by themselves, prohibiting or limiting the purchase of certain classes of North American goods. Almost every term of this description contains an ambiguity which we could argue about for hours; but it must serve.

There is no mystery about why such a state of affairs should have prevailed in Western Europe, including Britain, for some years after the war. Immense destruction had to be made good, disorganisation overcome, hunger and lassitude recuperated from. Primarily the dollar shortage was but one facet of a general shortage of productive power, aggravated, however, by the loss of precious sources of supply, beyond the Iron Curtain and in East Asia. With generous aid, some, though not all, of these troubles have been overcome, miracles effected, and the level of production almost everywhere raised well above pre-war level. Yet dollar shortage still persists. Why? And what to do about it?

And what has the Outer Sterling Area, mostly lying outside the War Zone, and turned, unlike Europe, from debtor into creditor, got to say for itself? Quite a bit, perhaps. It contains Malaya, gallantest of dollar-earners, but very much *in* the War Zone, and still hampered in its task of reconstruction by persistent and murderous guerrilla warfare. It contains India, her own frontiers indeed all but untouched by war, but her near-by sources of food-supply, Burma and Indonesia, floundering for years in chaos and bloodshed. More important still, from an accounting if not from a human point of view, it contains one huge and many smaller producers of gold, the one thing whose official dollar price has not risen at all since before the war. If the £370 million of gold sold by the Outer Area to Britain in 1946-9 could have been resold for dollars for only 40 per cent above the pre-war price, it would have wiped out the whole of the drain exercised by the Outer Area in those years on Britain's gold and dollar reserves.

To all such hard-luck stories there is one possible reply, and a good many people, both in America and elsewhere, have not failed to make it. What all this means, it can be said, is that the non-dollar, non-Soviet world was set by the war a stiff problem in readjustment. It was entitled to, and has received, generous help in tackling this problem. But if, after all these years, dollar shortage still persists, that means that this problem of readjustment has not been tackled with sufficient energy. Rather than tackle it, the more fully developed countries of the Eastern Hemisphere have clung tenaciously to ways of life and standards of consumption which they could no longer afford; the less developed ones have aimed at a pace of advance which they had no possible means of implementing. Balance could have been attained by now if the former had shaken off their crippling rigidities and the latter had toned down the exuberance of their visions. Given a breathing-space—and in this instance a breathing-space *has* been given—balance always *can* be attained between any two trading areas, however great the gap between them in productive power, provided that the less richly endowed area accepts the standard of life to which its relative efficiency entitles it, and does not keep kicking against the pricks by adhering obstinately to occupational immobility and utopian social policy, buttressed by monetary inflation and an over-valued exchange.

I think there is an immense amount of truth in this accusation. Speaking for myself, I can honestly say that I have always felt it to be the side of the truth on which a British economist was under obligation to lay special stress. It is five and a half years since, speaking as President of the Economic Section of the British Association for the Advancement of Science, I reminded my audience that "what are politely called 'balance of payment difficulties' do not necessarily drop like a murrain from heaven, but that any nation which gives its mind to it can create them for itself in half an hour with the aid of the printing press and a strong trade union movement". It has always seemed to me that until this simple truth was fully grasped and acted upon by the countries of Western Europe and the Sterling Area, it was much too early to frame permanent policies on the assumption that dollar shortage was an ineluctable condition of the world's affairs.

But I do not think this is the whole truth, or anything like it. That it cannot be the whole truth is suggested, if not by anything else, by the fact that dollar shortage is not a purely war-time or post-war phenomenon, but that traces of it, to put it mildly, can be found over the preceding quarter-century. The fact that the opposite side of the truth has often been put petulantly and ungenerously does not absolve me from drawing your attention to it, or you from giving it your candid consideration.

Let us go right back to the proposition that lies at the heart of the classical theory of international trade—the famous doctrine of comparative costs or comparative advantage. One country may be better endowed than another all round—with natural resources, with human skill, with an accumulated stock of capital instruments; yet in almost all circumstances unrestricted trade will be to the advantage of both. For the superiority of the first country over the second is virtually certain to be greater in some lines than in others, and it will pay it to concentrate on those lines in which its advantage is greatest, abandoning those in which its advantage is least to the weaker country. Provided the latter manages its monetary affairs properly, its inhabitants will only be conscious of a shortage of the stronger country's currency in the trivial sense in which they are conscious of a shortage of their own country's currency—each of them would be very glad to have more of it. It is just too bad that they have not; but as for remedial action, for the weaker country to seek to limit its commercial contacts with the stronger would simply be to cut off its own nose to spite its face.

What is wrong with this as a satisfying picture

of the relation between North America and the rest of the free world at the present time? There are three things wrong, I think the critics would say.

In the first place, it is essentially a static picture. What is to happen if country A is not only better endowed than country B, but if the disparity of endowment between them is continually *increasing* through the cumulative mutual interaction of capital accumulation and technological progress? It is true that at any given moment there will still be *some* distribution of function between the two countries which, if it could be instantaneously attained, would be in the best interests of both. But the task of attaining it, and then of abandoning it almost immediately for a new one, may surpass the human capacity for adjustment in what is, *ex hypothesi*, the weaker country. Better for it, so the argument runs, to be less tightly tied in the bonds of international trade, and to make what progress it can at its own pace. Let me illustrate in terms of the analogy with which it is common to bring home to elementary classes in economics the meaning of the doctrine of comparative advantage. The simple fellow who, to the advantage of both, has been earning a living by cooking the dinner for a busy and prosperous scientist wakes up one day to find that his master has invented a completely automatic cooker, and that if he wants to remain a member of the household he must turn shoeblack. He acquires a kit and learns the technique, only to find that his master has invented a dust-repelling shoe, but would nevertheless be graciously willing for him to remain on and empty the trash-bins. Would he not do better to remove himself from the orbit of the great man, and cultivate his own back garden? And if he can find some other simple fellows in the same case with whom to gang up and practise the division of labour on a less bewildering basis, so much the better for him. Such, it is urged, has become the position of the rest of the free world *vis-à-vis* the United States.

We may use the same personal analogy to illustrate the second ground on which the relevance to our present problem of the classical doctrine of comparative advantage has been questioned. One of the advantages of being well off is that one need not be in a tearing hurry to decide what to do next. In the words of the old song, one can stop, and look, and listen, without getting into an irretrievable mess. It is not only that the rich and clever scientist of my tale is always wanting some new service from his harassed employee; there are moments when, not having fully readjusted his own manner of life to his own discoveries, he is really wanting nothing at all. So is it when America stops and looks and listens, as she did in 1938 and again for a little while in 1949. She may be hardly conscious of the catch, so to speak, in her breath, but the countries of the Sterling Area know it all right, for a small percentage fall in her industrial activity generates a large percentage fall—by nearly a half in 1938, by a sixth even in 1949—in the value of her purchases from them, and reverberates like thunder right through the free world's economic system, intensifying dollar shortage from a sullen ache to a raging fever. Here, it is urged, is another reason for planning to detach oneself, so far as is possible, from her orbit.

You will notice that I have spoken only of 1938 and 1949. That is because I want to put "the case against America", if you like to call it that, reasonably and persuasively; and that is not done, I think, by harping on the years 1929 to 1932. That disaster was produced by a constellation of causes which may never recur, and aggravated by mistakes which *need* never recur. I have never been one of those who have built on it, as some of your own economists have done, a theory of the inevitable drift of modern capitalist economies towards a condition of chronic saturation and stagnation. But I find it hard to see how an economy like that of the United States is ever going to render itself immune from little hiccoughs of stock-taking and indecision like those of 1938 and 1949. I will go further and say that I am not at all sure that it is desirable that it should. For here too, as in the rest of the world, the social and political forces making for perpetual inflation are tremendously strong; and it may be that it is only through minor recessions of this kind that, even here, the reputation of money as a measure and store of value can be prevented from being irretrievably undermined. Nevertheless, as I have said, they have their inconveniences, to put it mildly, for the rest of us.

Dollar Shortage

The third cause of complaint cannot be adequately illustrated in terms of the brilliant scientist and his employee; indeed, it is just because it cannot that this cause of complaint exists. Let me explain. Countries are not homogeneous units, and, whether rich or poor, they suffer from schizophrenia in a way which individuals normally do not. If the law of comparative advantage is requiring a readjustment to be made for its fulfilment, there will always be people in both countries with a strong disposition to resist. Exporters will want to go on exporting what and whither they have been used to export; producers for a lucrative home market will object to seeing it, as they think, filched away from them. This is as true of the richer country as of the poorer one; it is as though there were one corner of the scientist's brain which urges him to go on blacking his own shoes, though the whole man is conscious that he would be more sensible not to. American shipping and shipbuilding interests, please note!

The richer the country the more easily it can afford, without doing serious harm to its own standard of life, to be tender to the vested interests which are resisting readjustment. By displaying such tenderness it increases the severity of the readjustment demanded of the poorer country, causing it, once more, to reflect whether the attainment of any kind of balance with the rich neighbour is not a hopeless quest—whether, to turn from the general to the particular, the cure for dollar shortage is not to be sought, not in trying to earn dollars but in training oneself resolutely to do without them.

Have I said enough to persuade you that when one of the partners to its operation is a country of multifarious resources and towering strength, the law of comparative advantage, for all its inexorable truth, needs a string of footnotes? That a quarrel and a baby are not the only things which it takes two to make, but that dollar shortage also falls within that interesting category? If so, we can go on to ask calmly what more America, who has poured forth a stream of generous gifts to help to set the world on its feet, can fairly be expected to do about it.

I will start by mentioning one thing which, in present circumstances at least, I do *not* think that she should be asked to do. I do not think she should be asked to consent to putting into operation the clause in the International Monetary Fund agreement which permits the nations, acting in concert, to raise their official buying-prices for gold. That clause was designed to meet a situation very different from that of the last few years—a situation in which it might plausibly be argued that a scarcity of the basic money metal was acting as a contributory cause of a long and savage deflation and depression like that of the early thirties. It would, in my view, be a misuse of it to put it into operation to re-stoke the fires of a world inflation. So far as equity goes, those who set out to produce a monetary metal are taking with their eyes open the opposite risk from those who set out to produce an ordinary commodity; they know that they stand to gain by a rise and to lose by a fall in the general purchasing power of the thing which they are co-operating to produce—money. It is hard luck if the game goes persistently against them, but it is not clear that they are morally entitled to any special relief. From a more practical standpoint, the free gift of dollar purchasing power which the United States would confer on the holders and producers of gold by raising her official buying-price would be distributed between countries in a way which would bear no close relation to need or to productive use. There are other and better ways in which to help.

Let me deal first, briefly and dogmatically, with some of the least controversial. First, it is America's international duty, as it is her own interest, so to operate her fiscal and monetary systems as to keep her economy so far as possible on an even keel. This does not mean that it is her duty to humour the rest of the world by leading it along a primrose path of perpetual inflation, under the influence of a perfectionist interpretation of that ambiguous and unfortunate phrase, full employment. But it does mean, I think, that in cases of doubt she is in a position to tilt the balance of her policy in an expansionist direction; for she can be free of those *arrière-pensées* about the effect of courageous action on the balance of payments by which the rest of us in similar conditions are bound to be beset.

Secondly, remembering how inevitably the throbs of her large industrial heart rock the world's boat, she can see to it that the pulsations are at least not aggravated by spasmodic and inconsiderate official action. If the Australians went out on the tiles in 1950, if Malaya's fight against Communism has been hampered by bewildering fluctuations in the price of her tin, the panicking and the tantrums of some of the United States purchasing agencies must bear, I think, no small share of the blame.

Thirdly, I believe that America's position imposes on her a special responsibility, above that of others, for grappling firmly with what I have called schizophrenia—the inevitable opposition of interested parties to structural change. The official policy enshrined in the Trade Agreement Acts, immense improvement as it has been on that which preceded it, does not really face up to this special responsibility. The emphasis is all on reciprocity and the extension of two-way trade—the problem of imbalance, little realised at the date (1934) of the original Act, finds no adequate recognition in its philosophy. This Act, together with that long overdue legislative simplification of Customs procedure which has hung fire so disappointingly since the crying need for it was publicly admitted in the autumn of 1949, may still prove the most convenient mechanism through which to put a more radical policy to work; but the policy must *be* more radical if any lasting progress is to be made in overcoming the disheartenment which so often attends the attempts of the European nations to pay their way. From among many possible and perhaps more entertaining illustrations I select just one, which struck me by its sober and matter-of-fact dignity. It is from a letter to *The Times* of May 2, 1952, by Mr. Foulkes, Managing Director of the Measuring and Scientific Equipment Company, London.

"We have the manufacturing facilities and the price-level that would make it attractive for us to sell to America, but the setting up of a suitable sales organisation over there, coupled with the necessity of stockage and servicing facilities in the United States under constant threat of increased tariffs, make this venture, attractive as it appears to us as a company and important as it must be from the national point of view, too risky and not a practical proposition."

Mr. Foulkes is not personally known to me, but his letter does not strike me as that of a timorous or unenterprising man.

In an important article in the *Economic Journal* for December 1951, the British economist, Donald MacDougall, whose writings are notably free from any kind of anti-American bias, has made the following points. Before the war the general level of wages in manufacturing industry was about twice as high in the United States as in Britain. In those industries in which the productivity of labour was more than twice as great in the United States as in Britain, the United States had the lion's share of the export market to third countries, and in those in which it was less than twice as great, Britain had the lion's share. This, of course, is exactly what we

65

should expect. But even in the latter range of industries Britain's exports *to the United States* were usually only a fraction of 1 per cent of the latter's consumption. The burden of the American tariff averaged twice as high—61 per cent as against 28 per cent—on those goods in which Britain had a comparative advantage as on those in which she had not, and in almost all cases offset or more than offset that comparative advantage. As MacDougall is careful to point out, the effective burden of some American tariff rates has been substantially reduced since the war, and the rise from 2 to 3½ in the ratio between the general levels of manufacturing wages in the two countries has probably not been fully offset by a corresponding rise in relative productivity. Hence the American tariff has become an instrument somewhat less beautifully fashioned than it used to be for defeating and frustrating the operation of the law of comparative advantage. But that there is room for further deterioration in this respect can scarcely be denied.

Let me not seem ungenerous about what has been recently achieved. Most Italian cheeses are no longer, since last July, a menace to the defence of the United States, though Canadian cheddar and Dutch Gouda remain somewhat dangerous—perhaps it is the cannon-ball-like shape of the latter which gives it its deadly quality. Under a let-out clause in the Buy American Act, an important electrical contract has been awarded by the Army to a British firm, though it needed a gap of £63,000 in the tender price to ensure this. Mr. Truman's re-jection of the claims of the garlic-growers, the watchmakers, the motor-cycle makers for increased protection under the escape clause of the Trade Agreement Act was decisive and firmly phrased, though he still thought it necessary to lay a stress on the importance of maintaining the total volume of American exports which, if politically astute, was educationally misleading. We are grateful—and we ask for more, much more.

Fourthly, America, which includes in this con-text Americans in international service, can be asked to continue and expand her efforts to re-create the stream of private long-term overseas investment, and to experiment with methods of supplementing it. It is not her fault, though it is the world's mis-fortune, that she has not hitherto had, save only in respect to oil, the same compelling motive as Britain had in her nineteenth-century creditor days for assisting to open up all over the world new sources of food and raw material supply. It may be —though I have heard it questioned—that, as fore-shadowed in the remarkable report rendered to President Truman by his Raw Materials Commis-sion last June, the Paley Report, this situation will change drastically over the next quarter-century, and the self-interest of American industry impel it to embark on a huge programme, amounting to hundreds of millions of dollars a year, of exploita-tion of, at any rate, *mineral* resources overseas. That will be all to the good as far as it goes; but such a development, if it occurs, will bring its own problems. It is by no means true that such enterprises do not benefit the populations among whom they are conducted; nevertheless, there is evidently a certain danger of their becoming islands of high wages and high consumption standards, imperfectly integrated with the much more primitive life around them, and disruptive as well as educative in their social effects. It is not good that a backward country should be dependent for its basic services of power, communication, health and the like on the ancillary activities of particular private empires, however enlightened; and the fate of the Anglo-Iranian Oil Company, which to the best of my knowledge did the job about as well as it can be done, may stand as a warning. It is worth remembering, as Professor Nurkse of Columbia University has recently reminded us, that when British overseas investments were at their zenith in 1914, only a quarter of them in nominal capital value (though admittedly this was the most lucrative section in annual income) consisted of mines, plantations and the like; the remaining three-quarters, even in those so-called laissez-faire days, consisted of railways and other public utilities and of loans to Governments which were themselves operating schemes of basic development—roads, harbours, irrigation-works and so forth. It would seem that somehow or other a balanced policy of overseas investment by the world's greatest creditor nation must, under political conditions admittedly more difficult than those of the nineteenth century, be so fashioned as to include provision for these things, and for the slow processes of agricultural improvement, and not be confined to the sucking of petroleum and the tearing of metals out of the bowels of the earth.

Perhaps in saying this I am going a little beyond my theme; for from the point of view of immediate closure of the dollar gap one act of long-term foreign investment is as good as another, and from the point of view of narrowing it in the future an act of investment which directly generates a flood of exportable petroleum or bauxite may clearly be more efficacious than one which does not. Certainly I do not mean either to decry what is called "direct" investment, or to advocate—a vain enough task—that American investors, forgetting the lessons of the 1920s, should rush to finance overseas schemes of municipal extravagance or mushroom industry which can only add to the balance of payments difficulties of the countries which indulge in them. All I am suggesting is that this delicate problem of the channelling of capital from richer countries into poorer ones has many facets and needs approaching by many complementary routes, among which loans to Governments of proved stability and integrity is still one. And it is to be hoped that a high percentage of the total number of such Governments will continue to be found, as it has been in the past, within the Sterling Area.

In these respects of comprehensiveness of outlook and elasticity of approach the pioneering work which has been done, under American leadership, by the International Bank for Reconstruction and Development seems to me deserving of the highest praise. But of course the rate of some $200 million a year at which it is at present able, consistently with its rules and standards, to disburse its own funds and those which it gathers from the market is not high compared with the $3½ billion at which the current surplus of the United States, reckoned on the narrowest basis,[1] stood in 1951, still less as compared with the fantastic annual figure of $10 billion at which the so-called experts of the United Nations have assessed the needs of the so-called undeveloped countries of the earth for foreign capital —"those undeveloped countries from whose bourn no capital returns", as Shakespeare has so eloquently put it. The problem of working out the scope and the technique of a programme of foreign investment which is not too large to be acceptable to the investors and tax-payers of the lending countries or assimilable by the borrowing countries, and is at the same time large enough to make a real hole in the problem of dollar shortage, remains most formidable.

[1] I.e. after deduction of private gifts and of munitions sent as Military Aid, as well as deducting military expenditures overseas.

IV

Discrimination

I COME now to what is to my mind intellectually, if
not practically, a much more difficult matter. What
line is America to take about collective attempts by
other countries to ease their own problems by imposing on her exports restrictions greater than any
they impose on trade between themselves? A few
years ago the reply of American official opinion
would have been unanimous and emphatic. All such
discriminatory arrangements are the work of the
devil and must be resisted, not only as a matter of
self-interest, but as a high moral duty. One exception only can be allowed; if two or more countries
abolish *all* restrictions between themselves, becoming for commercial purposes one country, they can
be allowed, like any other country, to impose
reasonable restrictions on imports from the outside
world. That answer has never satisfied other countries, and is nowadays given less confidently even in
this.

Let us look at this complicated and delicate matter
as calmly as we can, starting with pure economics,
and with the economics of a normal world, in which
no loud cries of dollar shortage or pound shortage or
franc shortage are being heard. Three countries,

which we will call Britain, France and America, are each of them imposing impartial restrictions of one kind or another on imports from the other two. Britain and France now abolish all restrictions between themselves, and unify, at a level on balance no more aggressive than before, their restrictions against America. What will be the result? The answer which I shall give is the passage which I warned you in my first lecture might be a little difficult to follow, though it is, I am afraid, a great simplification of what might, and perhaps ought to, be said. It seems that any one of at least four things, or some mixture of the four, might happen. First, Britain and France may now make for each other things which each of them, while mutual restrictions were in force, found it cheaper to import from America. This will be bad for America, and bad, though they may persuade themselves otherwise, for themselves; for each will now be drawing on a dearer instead of a cheaper source of supply. Secondly, Britain and France may now make for each other things which each of them used to make less efficiently for itself, and may go on buying from America just what they used to buy; this will be good for them and do no harm to her. Thirdly, taking a more dynamic view, this better division of labour between Britain and France may reveal to them such glorious possibilities of satisfying each other's wants that their desire for American goods declines, and the productive resources which used to be employed in making exports to pay for them are diverted to other purposes. This will be bad for America, but not necessarily for the three countries viewed as an archangel might view them, that is to say, as a single whole. Fourthly, still taking a dynamic view, the better division of labour between Britain and France may release so much productive energy in both countries that, in addition to ministering better to each other's needs, they become more efficient producers for the American market and keener customers for American goods. This will be good for everybody concerned.

From this analysis three important points emerge. First, an outcome which is against the interest of "America" *may* be against the interest of the whole world if that is rightly judged; but it may not. Secondly, whether we take "America's" point of view or the world's, it is not at all obvious that in a case where a 100 per cent union between "Britain" and "France" would produce on balance a good result, a lesser degree of union—say a system of preferential tariffs—would produce a bad one. It will only do so if it is specially framed to foster harmful changes in the direction of trade, whereas a 100 per cent union would have been unselective between harmful changes and salutary ones. Thirdly, the condition most likely to produce a truly good result for the combining countries—whether or not it turns out also to be good for "America"—is that their industries to start with should be highly similar and therefore competitive, but that there should be between them great unexplored potentialities of diversification and therefore of co-operation. There is not much point in closer union between countries either if they are highly complementary and co-operative already, or if there is no possibility of their being made so.

Now, with these points in mind, let us look at the two groups towards which, in the real world, the United States is called upon to take up an attitude—the Sterling Area and those countries of Western Continental Europe which, associated with Britain first as beneficiaries of Marshall Aid and now as partners in the European Payments Union, have also been taking partial and spasmodic initiatives towards other forms of closer association. Still speaking economically, and still keeping dollar shortage in the background, how do these two groups shape as candidates, so to speak, for the privileges of discriminatory union?

By no means perfectly, as it seems to me, either of them—but for opposite reasons. Between the major elements of the Sterling Area—the industrial mother-country, the agricultural temperate-zone Dominions, the tropical dependencies and ex-dependencies—there is already a high degree of differentiation and complementarity—that is how the Area came into existence originally. Possibly behind the protection of a ring-fence it *might* prove a little easier to repress some exuberant growths of local uneconomic nationalism, especially in the Antipodes, and to exploit some hitherto unexploited possibilities of mutual service, always provided—

and it is a big proviso—that capital to finance the exploitation would consent to flow in on an adequate scale from outside the fence. But the possibilities are limited, and the dangers real that behind the protection of the ring-fence the constituent elements of the Area should lie back on the feather-bed of the easy mutual trade with one another, and not pursue with sufficient ardour those more difficult contacts with the outside world which hold greater potentialities for raising their standard of life. Whether given out of self-interest or goodwill or a mixture of both, the lectures on this topic which reach us Sterlingarians from North America deserve in my view to be taken well to heart. And in North America I include Northern North America, once our fellow-conspirator in the Ottawa Conference of 1932 where Imperial Preference was brought to birth, now more prominent as our co-mentor—and let me add co-benefactor—with the United States. About Imperial Preference itself I shall have a little more to say in a moment from other points of view. For the moment let me sum up by saying that as a congeries of countries between which business contacts are close, means of payment easy and exchange stability probable if not assured, the Sterling Area seems to me to have a great and innocuous future; as a candidate for a permanent ring-fence I think its claims are low—if only because of the utter impossibility, so often conveniently forgotten by the fence-builders in my country, of bringing Canada within the ring.

And now what about Europe? Let me confess that Englishmen have found it rather puzzling to reconcile the reserve, to put it mildly, with which American opinion has always regarded the phenomena of Imperial Preference and the Sterling Area with the enthusiasm and insistence which it has displayed in these last few years in pressing on Western Europe the idea of closer union. For some years the contradiction was to some extent veiled behind the convention to which I have already alluded, namely, that a 100 per cent union is necessarily good for all concerned while anything less than 100 per cent is necessarily bad. For what was pressed on Europe at first was a complete Customs Union. But under the modern conditions of elaborate and far-reaching Government intervention in internal economic affairs which prevail even in so-called liberal countries like Belgium, Italy and Germany and to a greater degree in more socialistically minded ones, it has become pretty clear that this concept of a Customs Union is not really a very helpful one. Great difficulties have been found in giving real economic content to the Customs Union which has now for five years been in nominal existence between Holland and Belgium, while those which were at one time projected between France and Italy and between the Scandinavian countries have failed to achieve even nominal birth. It is true that there has just been set on foot an experiment in complete union in respect of certain industries— those of coal and steel—between France, Germany, the Low Countries and Italy. It is a most interesting experiment, which will deserve careful watching. I can only say that at present I am not persuaded it is likely to work in such a manner as to upset the conclusion that complete economic union between the countries of Western Europe is not achievable in advance of a political union which is not yet above the horizon. I hope I am right in believing that American official opinion has now become more realistic about this, and is prepared to interpret such high-sounding words as "union" and "integration" in a more modest way, covering in the first place certain definite military arrangements which fall outside my purview, and secondly such things as the mutual reduction of trade restrictions and the use of a common payments mechanism, with such other practical but unspectacular methods of mutual help as the ingenious and efficient staff of the Organisation for European Economic Co-operation in Paris has been able to devise. And this retreat from perfectionism has, I am sure, been wise; there is no reason why, if the whole would have been *very* good, the part should not be made *rather* good, not positively bad. But America's recognition of this truth with respect to Europe makes more rather than less glaring the contrast with her official attitude towards the preferential arrangements of the British Commonwealth and the Sterling Area.

What is the reason for this difference of attitude? Is it purely political and strategic? Or is there also economic justification for it? Well, I think there is *some*. Let us go back to our formulation of the condition favourable for the evolution of a beneficent discriminatory or preferential system. It was, you will remember, that the economic systems of the countries concerned must be *actually* highly competitive but *potentially* highly complementary or co-operative. There is probably more actual uneconomic competition between the countries of Western Europe than between those of the Sterling Area—more scope therefore for energy-releasing preferential arrangements, which will redound to the advantage of the countries concerned and possibly also in the long run, though not certainly, to that of the rest of the world. On the other hand, it is easy to exaggerate the degree of complementarity that is likely to be attainable by such methods. Fundamentally, it would seem, the nations of Western Europe are doomed to a high degree of mutual competition. Within many pairs or triads of the constituent countries there are bound to be large groups of people who are trying to make a living in much the same way, and wanting much the same things from the world overseas. That is why it does not do to expect too much in the way of beneficent re-distribution of economic activity from projects of Western European economic union, whether partial or complete. It is also why such projects carry with them certain insidious dangers. One is the danger of degenerating into projects for bigger and better cartels between the producers, in different lands, of inevitably similar articles—for instance the French and Italian producers of vegetables. The other is the danger that, so far as specialism between countries *is* encouraged, it will be specialism in pleasant luxuries for mutual consumption rather than in things which contribute to the whole area's power of earning its essential requirements from overseas. There is a certain risk, as I once put it in a broadcast talk, of the countries of Europe developing "into a lot of old flower-women, each pestering the others to buy her early violets, and all finding themselves without the means to buy their daily bread". All things considered, I am not sure that on general economic grounds Western Europe is really a much stronger candidate than the British Commonwealth or the Sterling Area for the new-found American tolerance towards preferential groupings.

It seems to me that in both cases the grounds for asking for that tolerance are much the same. In neither case can the request be securely based on those general considerations which have led official American opinion in the past to make in favour of the Customs Union an exception to its general doctrine of non-discrimination. In both cases the request must be based partly on the reality of the phenomenon described as dollar shortage, partly on considerations which are rather political than economic. Let me develop these points in that order.

What difference does dollar shortage make? It means surely that, if it is a sufficiently real and acute thing to justify other countries in putting restrictions on imports from dollar countries to protect their gold and dollar reserves, there is nothing to be gained from a world point of view in compelling them to impose equivalent restrictions on trade between themselves. Let me not be ungenerous; there has been recognition of this truth in practice, in America's treatment of the Sterling Area as well as of Europe; but it has had to be won at the expense of one disastrously premature experiment in freedom in 1947, and of a constant pressure on the British Authorities, not conducive to good morals or good feeling, to pay lip-service to principles inadequately thought out in their application to current circumstances.

Let me say again that I think the policies of Britain and most of the Sterling Area countries in the post-war years have been faulty in many respects, based on false monetary doctrines and perverted interpretations of the concept of full employment. Let me say again that I do not see any way out for these countries along the lines of a self-sufficient, high-cost fenced area, even if the fence could be extended, as some of its would-be architects now seem to be ready to contemplate, to include the Western European countries and their dependencies on some kind of at present ill-defined lower platform. I am convinced that it is the duty and true interest of all these countries to take sincere, speedy and energetic steps towards the establishment of a much freer and less discriminating system. But since I think the problem of dollar shortage is in some measure bilateral, I believe that one of the contributions that can fairly be asked for from America towards its handling is a more explicitly good-humoured and tolerant—a less theological—attitude towards such differentiations in commercial treatment as may yet remain. And since I think the problem has long-run or at least recurrent elements as well as purely temporary ones, I would not myself care to talk in terms which suggest that the day of complete and irreversible non-discrimination is much, if any, nearer than the day of complete free trade.

On the political side I am driven to very similar conclusions. The political and strategic arguments for encouraging closer cohesion between the countries of Western Europe need no development from me. As regards the Commonwealth, like many other Englishmen brought up in the liberal tradition, I regarded what was done at Ottawa in 1932 without enthusiasm, and in particular with a strong consciousness of the danger of preferential systems being used to the damage of dependent territories in the interest of obsolescent metropolitan industries. But, apart altogether from the glaring illogicality of the exception claimed by the United States for her relationship with Cuba, I have never been able to see that there is any moral force in the view that federation between things which have hitherto been called States, or the absorption into such a Federation of vast slices of new territory, justifies a considerable degree of joint discrimination against foreigners, while territories which find a lower degree of political union more convenient are to be debarred from exercising any discrimination at all. I suppose this is a matter in which the very different history of our two countries inevitably colours their respective political imaginations. The American is used to the idea of certain definite possible conflicts between State and Federal rights which have to be resolved somehow, but he has no doubt that his country is the United States, and that the United States is, not are, his country. The Englishman has long been used to living in a certain haze as to what his country is—whether England or England-and-Wales or Great Britain or the United Kingdom of Great Britain and Northern Ireland or the United Kingdom plus its dependent territories or that larger unit which he used to call the British Empire and is now told that, unless he happens to be Mr. Churchill, he had better call the British Commonwealth or even just the Commonwealth. He used to think he knew the difference between a self-governing Dominion and a colony, but now each year he is increasingly hard put to it to tell t'other from which. Himself an ardent monarchist, he is getting used to the idea that he has a special political bond with many millions of people who are citizens of a republic, and he knows that in some queer way even Irishmen manage to be simultaneously both foreigners and non-foreigners. It is not unnatural that he should feel that these complex political relationships can receive, no less legitimately than the simple relationship between a New Yorker and a

Virginian, some economic expression and sanction.

I believe it would be well worth America's while to make an effort of the imagination towards taking a different view of all this. I do not think her attempt to put and keep the "elimination" of imperial preference in the forefront of the plan presented to England, in the hour of her mortal peril, for the better ordering of the world, was a very wise act. I suspect that until the day when all agricultural tariffs and farm-support policies are consigned to the dustbin, she might even be wise to acquiesce in such tidyings-up of the General Agreement on Tariffs and Trade as may be necessary to reconcile a reasonable British agricultural policy with the principle of free entry into Britain of foodstuffs from the Commonwealth overseas: though I confess that this was not one of the proposals of the recent Commonwealth Economic Conference which as an old Free Trader I personally regarded with much enthusiasm.

Would a franker revision of United States ideology on these matters be liable to be abused? It is impossible to predict with certainty. That there are people in my country who would think it right to do what I should consider abusing it, I have already admitted. But I think there are strong forces limiting their ability to do so. I have already more than once called attention to the momentous lack of correspondence in membership between the old imperial preferential system and the new Sterling Area—impairing, as it seems to me, the power of both to act as breeding-grounds for any very sinister developments. That strapping young lady Canada, though she has rightly called a mountain by Mr. Amery's name and though she sent us years ago the ambiguous gift of Lord Beaverbrook, has shown very little inclination to dance to either of their pipings. And there are other grown-up young ladies, fair and dark, who though, as I have said, they get more out of the sterling system than they are always ready to admit, can be relied on to resist its degradation into a permanent feather-bed for indolent British manufacturers. As for the colonial peoples, well for some of them, notably the sugar-growers in the Caribbean, the sterling-cum-preferential system has clearly been on balance not an oppressive tyrant but a fairy godmother, protecting, at the expense of the British consumer, the only sure way of earning a livelihood they have yet been able to discover. It may be possible—that is what I should like to see—for these rival preferential systems in the Caribbean —yours and ours—to be merged some day in a more truly international and constructive scheme for handling this difficult sugar problem than has yet been evolved; my point is simply that meanwhile they can neither of them be condemned out of hand as instruments of exploitation. Elsewhere, in Africa and Asia, vigilance is still in my view required to prevent the preferential system from becoming a means of withholding from the colonial peoples the benefit of cheap textiles and other goods, and the sterling system from becoming the means of too-easy borrowing by the mother-country when she is in difficulties. With the recent rapid development of self-government in West Africa, and the strong and persistent pressure for increased African participation in the government of the plural societies in other parts of the continent, a plentiful supply of local and vocal watchdogs can be confidently counted upon, though they may still need both assistance and criticism from liberal opinion elsewhere. In ten or twenty years the African consumer may be in less danger of exploitation by Lancashire or Bombay than by local manufacturing interests thrown up by the prevailing pressure for high-speed industrialisation.

As regards American interests in these dependent territories, I would not like to try, as in some quarters has been done, to emphasise and exploit the divergence of view which in times of difficulty may always arise between the creditor interests of a powerful country and its exporting interests, the former thinking it more important that scarce foreign exchange should be used for the remittance of interest payments, the latter for the purchase of goods. I would rather take the broader ground that all American citizens have an overriding interest in the orderly evolution of these parts of the world through the progressive development therein of real and cordial relations of partnership between the British and the African peoples. It seems to me doubtful if that American interest would be furthered by clamour for the complete disruption of the Commonwealth preferential system, still less of the Sterling Area.

You will be telling me that I have forgotten the subject of my lectures, and that instead of informing you about Britain's position in the world economy, I am doing nothing but preach to you about America's duty in the same. But in truth the subjects *are* closely intermingled. In particular, much of what I said just now about the limitations of Western Europe as a candidate for economic union is relevant to the topic which I have not yet directly discussed, and to which I propose to devote my remaining minutes, namely, Britain's own relations with that area. For the same reasons which make it important that America should not expect too much from schemes of European integration go far to explain why Britain has not been able to throw herself so unreservedly into such schemes as some of her American and Continental critics would have liked. There are, of course, enormous opportunities for beneficial exchange of goods and services between Britain and her Continental neighbours; but no degree of intimate union with them could make up to her for any loss of freedom of contact with the great granaries, pastures, minefields and plantations overseas from which she draws the essential nutriment for the stomachs of her people and of her factories. The reservations which she would be bound to make to keep those life-lines intact would make her an uneasy and indeed impossible bedfellow in any close scheme of European economic union, whose prospects of success would only therefore be impaired rather than improved by her attempted inclusion.

This is a matter in which English party politics have done some damage, now it is to be hoped in process of rectification. Some members of the late Socialist Administration, wedded to ambitious schemes of national planning, thought it necessary to proclaim somewhat loudly their inability to visualise close association with countries with a different ideological outlook from their own; and the late Conservative Opposition, or one wing of it, tried to cash in on this situation by joining in the cry that England was dragging her feet and hinting that much more was to be expected from an alternative Government. But when that Government duly arrived, it adopted in practice much the same attitude as its predecessor, as indeed any British Government, but perhaps especially one drawn from a party with a long tradition of being the party of Empire, is bound to do. Hence some disappointment and disillusion, which it has taken some wise statesmanship on the part of our present Foreign Secretary and Chancellor of the Exchequer to allay.

In point of fact there has been very little dragging of feet under either Government. It was our Mr. Bevin who in 1947 took the initiative in responding to General Marshall's overtures, our Sir Oliver Franks who guided and inspired that hastily convoked committee whose report has been summarised in a poem which I must not stop to quote in full, but which ends with the couplet:

Then look benignly on your zealous scholars,
Dear Mr. Marshall, and release the dollars.

Ever since then British civil servants and technical experts have played a prominent part in all the constructive work of the O.E.E.C.—in particular, in the intricate task of so interweaving the pre-existing system of sterling payments through London with the new and complicated structure of the European Payments Union centred at Basle as to enable the latter to ease the mechanism of payments over a far larger area of the world than would otherwise have been possible. Again, in the movement for the mutual reduction of barriers to intra-European trade, Britain co-operated to an extent which was one of the chief immediate causes of her exchange crisis in 1951; and when she was forced to draw back, she did so with greater consideration for the exporting interests of her European sisters than was shown to her by one at least of her own daughters. There have been times during the last few years when she has had a good deal of reason to feel like Cordelia, less gifted than some who could be named at heaving her heart into her mouth, but not backward at helpful action.

Let me give one illustration of the way in which Britain's many-faceted position may subject her to conflicting pressures. You may remember that in my second lecture I pointed out that for any resident in the United Kingdom or the rest of the Sterling Area the pound is already "convertible" into dollars in the sense that, to pay for any authorised import from the United States, he can buy dollars or, what comes to the same thing, transfer sterling to the holder of an American sterling account. This right does not extend to Continental holders of sterling; and during last summer there arose from the Continent a strong cry, backed by a number of important interests in the City of London, that Britain should make a stout and speedy effort to make the pound "convertible", even if necessary at a fluctuating rate of exchange, in the sense of extending these rights of transfer, at least for the purpose of making payment for current imports, to Continental and presumably other foreign holders of sterling. It sounds at first hearing an attractive programme, from a Dominion and an American as well as from a Continental point of view—there is much magic in a word. But what if such a programme could only be safely attempted to the accompaniment of a sharp stiffening of the restrictions on the import of dollar goods to which those whose sterling is already "convertible" are subjected? Is that what the Dominions really mean by convertibility of the pound? Is it what America means? I do not think so. The plain truth is that while technical convertibility and the removal of import restrictions may both be important ultimate objects of policy, they may of necessity be in the meantime to some extent alternative or rival lines of advance, in the sense that if there is to be a larger move along one of them, there will have to be a smaller move along the other. And I fancy that in giving, as it becomes possible, the relaxation of import restrictions parity with or even priority over a progressive movement towards technical "convertibility", Britain would be meeting America's true desires as well as following her own best interests, even if it means that murmurs about dragging the feet continue to be heard from across the North Sea. Somewhat cryptic as they are, I take the allusions to this topic in the communiqués issued at the time of the Commonwealth Conference in December and at the close of the Washington talks a fortnight ago to indicate that that view has prevailed. If so, it is by no means all sections of European opinion who will be disappointed. In particular, those who are concerned with the working of the Organisation for European Economic Co-operation have evidently been in a state of some concern lest a unilateral dash for convertibility on the part of Britain should lead her to stiffen up her restrictions on the import of goods from the Continent, and should disrupt that ingenious piece of mechanism, the European Payments Union, which, while limited in its geographic coverage, does now oil the wheels of trade and finance over a very large part of the world's surface.

My hosts, I thank you for the patience with which you have listened to my attempts at an analysis of these difficult problems. When, more than a year ago, I selected them as the subject of my lectures, I did not of course know that a fortnight before my debt fell due they would also have been the subject of discussions at the highest level between the leading statesmen and experts of our two countries. I must confess that ever since I read that that meeting in Washington was to take place, I have been haunted by the fear lest it should lead to agreement so complete, and to announcements so enlightened and comprehensive, that I should have no option but to tear up my script and cable a last-minute cancellation of my acceptance of your invitation. Well, the communiqué was not such as to compel me to take those distasteful steps. But I need not tell you how fervently I hope, as I am sure you do likewise, that it will be seen in retrospect to have signified the beginning of a new and sustained attempt, on the part of all concerned, to set these matters on a better footing, and thus to cement the strength and promote the happiness of the free world.

INDEX

For Product Safety Concerns and Information please contact our EU
representative GPSR@taylorandfrancis.com Taylor & Francis Verlag GmbH,
Kaufingerstraße 24, 80331 München, Germany

Printed and bound by CPI Group (UK) Ltd, Croydon, CR0 4YY
08/05/2025
01864370-0002